C000008384

ACCEPTING OTHERS

Jesus said,
"I have set you
an example that you
should do as I have
done for you."

John 13:15

God's Words of Life on
ANXIETY

Be strong and courageous. Do not
be terrified; do not be discouraged,
for the LORD your God will be with
you wherever you go.

Joshua 1:9

The LORD is with you when you are
with him. If you seek him, he will
be found by you.

2 Chronicles 15:2

God's Words of Life on

ANXIETY

Do not be anxious about anything,
but in everything, by prayer and
petition, with thanksgiving, present
your requests to God. And the
peace of God, which transcends
all understanding, will guard
your hearts and your minds in
Christ Jesus.

Philippians 4:6–7

The LORD gives
strength to his people;
the LORD blesses
his people with peace.

Psalm 29:11

[A wife of noble character] is
    clothed with strength and dignity;
    she can laugh at the days to come.
She speaks with wisdom,
    and faithful instruction is on
    her tongue.

Proverbs 31:25–26

God has made everything beautiful in
its time.

Ecclesiastes 3:11

God's Words of Life on
BEAUTY

Your beauty should not come from
outward adornment, such as braided
hair and the wearing of gold jewelry
and fine clothes. Instead, it should
be that of your inner self, the
unfading beauty of a gentle and
quiet spirit, which is of great worth

in God's sight. For this is the way
the holy women of the past who
put their hope in God used to make
themselves beautiful.

1 Peter 3:3–5

God's Words of Life on
CONFLICT

Live in harmony with one another;
be sympathetic . . . be compassionate and humble. Do not repay
evil with evil or insult with insult,
but with blessing, because to this
you were called so that you may
inherit a blessing.

1 Peter 3:8–9

God's Words of Life on
CONFLICT

If your brother sins against you,
go and show him his fault, just
between the two of you. If he
listens to you, you have won
your brother over.

Matthew 18:15

Starting a quarrel is like breaching
    a dam;
    so drop the matter before a
    dispute breaks out.

Proverbs 17:14

God's Words of Life on
CONTENTMENT

Better the little that the righteous have
   than the wealth of many wicked;
for the power of the wicked will be
      broken,
   but the LORD upholds the
      righteous.

Psalm 37:16–17

Better one handful with tranquility
   than two handfuls with toil
   and chasing after the wind.

Ecclesiastes 4:6

CONTENTMENT

I know what it is to be in need,
and I know what it is to have
plenty. I have learned the secret of
being content in any and every
situation, whether well fed or hungry, whether living in plenty or in
want. I can do everything through
Christ who gives me strength.

Philippians 4:12–13

God's Words of Life on
CREATIVITY

We have different gifts, according to the grace given us. If a man's gift is prophesying, let him use it in proportion to his faith. If it is serving, let him serve; if it is teaching, let him teach; if it is encouraging, let him encourage; if it is contributing to the needs of others, let him give generously; if it is leadership, let him govern diligently; if it is showing mercy, let him do it cheerfully.

Romans 12:6–8

God's Words of Life on
DEPRESSION

Let the morning bring me word of
your unfailing love, Lord,
for I have put my trust in you.
Show me the way I should go,
for to you I lift up my soul.

Psalm 143:8

God's Words of Life on
DEPRESSION

The LORD is a refuge for the
oppressed,
a stronghold in times of trouble.

Psalm 9:9

The eternal God is your refuge,
and underneath are the
everlasting arms.

Deuteronomy 33:27

"I will build [my people] up and not
tear them down; I will plant them
and not uproot them. I will give
them a heart to know me, that I am
the LORD. They will be my people,
and I will be their God, for they
will return to me with all their
heart," says the Lord.

Jeremiah 24:6–7

God's Words of Life on

DISAPPOINTMENT

In you our fathers put their trust, Lord;
    they trusted and you delivered them.
They cried to you and were saved;
    in you they trusted and were not
    disappointed.

Psalm 22:4–5

Trust in him at all times,
O people;
pour out your hearts
to him,
for God is our refuge.

Psalm 62:8

DISCIPLESHIP

I have been crucified with Christ and I no longer live, but Christ lives in me. The life I live in the body, I live by faith in the Son of God, who loved me and gave himself for me.

Galatians 2:20

Jesus said, "By this all men will know that you are my disciples, if you love one another."

John 13:35

Jesus replied, "If anyone loves me, he will obey my teaching. My Father will love him, and we will come to him and make our home with him."

John 14:23

God's Words of Life on

ENCOURAGEMENT

May our Lord Jesus Christ himself
and God our Father, who loved
us and by his grace gave us eternal
encouragement and good hope,
encourage your hearts and
strengthen you in every good
deed and word.

2 Thessalonians 2:16–17

God's Words of Life on
ENCOURAGEMENT

My soul finds rest in God alone;
my salvation comes from him.
He alone is my rock and my
salvation;
he is my fortress, I will never
be shaken.

Psalm 62:1–2

God's Words of Life on
ENCOURAGEMENT

Yet this I call to mind
    and therefore I have hope:
Because of the LORD'S great love
    we are not consumed,
    for his compassions never fail.
They are new every morning;
    great is your faithfulness.

Lamentations 3:21–23

Why are you downcast, O my soul?
Why so disturbed within me?
Put your hope in God,
for I will yet praise him,
my Savior and my God.

Psalm 42:5–6

God's Words of Life on
ETERNAL LIFE

God has given us eternal life, and
this life is in his Son. He who has
the Son has life.

1 John 5:11–12

For God so loved the world that he
gave his one and only Son, that
whoever believes in him shall not
perish but have eternal life.

John 3:16

Surely goodness and love
will follow me
all the days of my life,
and I will dwell
in the house of the
LORD forever.

Psalm 23:6

FAITH

Now faith is being sure of what
we hope for and certain of what
we do not see.

Hebrews 11:1

Faith comes from hearing the
message, and the message is heard
through the word of Christ.

Romans 10:17

Jesus replied, "I tell you the truth, if you have faith as small as a mustard seed, you can say to this mountain, 'Move from here to there' and it will move. Nothing will be impossible for you."

Matthew 17:20

God's Words of Life on
FINANCES

Jesus said, "Provide purses for yourselves that will not wear out, a
treasure in heaven that will not be
exhausted, where no thief comes
near and no moth destroys. For
where your treasure is, there your
heart will be also."

Luke 12:33–34

Give, and it will be given to you.
A good measure, pressed down,
shaken together and running over,
will be poured into your lap. For
with the measure you use, it will be
measured to you.

Luke 6:38

Let no debt
remain outstanding,
except the continuing
debt to love one another,
for he who loves
his fellowman has
fulfilled the law.

Romans 13:8

If we confess our sins, God is
faithful and just and will forgive
us our sins and purify us from
all unrighteousness.

1 John 1:9

When you stand praying, if you
hold anything against anyone,
forgive him, so that your Father in
heaven may forgive you your sins.

Mark 11:25

God's Words of Life on
FORGIVENESS

"Come now, let us reason together,"
   says the LORD.
"Though your sins are like scarlet,
   they shall be as white as snow;
though they are red as crimson,
   they shall be like wool."

   Isaiah 1:18

Be kind and
compassionate to
one another,
forgiving each other,
just as in Christ God
forgave you.

Ephesians 4:32

God's Words of Life on
FRIENDSHIP

A friend loves at all times.

Proverbs 17: 17

Jesus said, "I no longer call you servants, because a servant does not know his master's business. Instead, I have called you friends, for everything that I learned from my Father I have made known to you."

John 15:15

FRIENDSHIP

Perfume and incense bring joy
    to the heart,
      and the pleasantness of one's friend
        springs from his earnest counsel.

Proverbs 27:9

There is a friend who sticks closer
    than a brother.

Proverbs 18:24

FRUSTRATION

Let us acknowledge the LORD;
    let us press on to acknowledge
    him.
As surely as the sun rises,
    he will appear;
he will come to us like the winter
    rains,
    like the spring rains that water
    the earth.

Hosea 6:3

And we know
that in all things
God works for the
good of those who love
him, who have been
called according to
his purpose.

Romans 8:28

No discipline
seems pleasant at the
time, but painful.
Later on, however, it
produces a harvest of
righteousness and peace
for those who have
been trained by it.

Hebrews 12:11

For God did not send his Son
into the world to condemn the
world, but to save the world
through him. Whoever believes
in him is not condemned.

John 3:17–18

God's Words of Life on
GRACE

When the kindness and love of God our Savior appeared, he saved us, not because of righteous things we had done, but because of his mercy. He saved us through the washing of rebirth and renewal by the Holy Spirit, whom he poured out on us generously through Jesus

Christ our Savior, so that, having
been justified by his grace, we
might become heirs having the
hope of eternal life.

Titus 3:4–7

God's Words of Life on

GRACE

Let us draw near to God with a sincere heart in full assurance of faith, having our hearts sprinkled to cleanse us from a guilty conscience and having our bodies washed with pure water. Let us hold unswervingly to the hope we profess, for he who promised is faithful.

Hebrews 10:22–23

GRIEF AND DEATH

Multitudes who sleep in the dust of the earth will awake: some to everlasting life. . . . Those who are wise will shine like the brightness of the heavens, and those who lead many to righteousness, like the stars for ever and ever.

Daniel 12:2–3

Listen, I tell you a mystery: We will
not all sleep, but we will all be
changed—in a flash, in the twin-
kling of an eye, at the last trumpet.
For the trumpet will sound, the
dead will be raised imperishable,
and we will be changed. For the
perishable must clothe itself with
the imperishable, and the mortal
with immortality. When the perishable has been clothed with the

imperishable, and the mortal with immortality, then the saying that is written will come true: "Death has been swallowed up in victory." "Where, O death, is your victory? Where, O death, is your sting?"

1 Corinthians 15:51–55

God's Words of Life on
GRIEF AND DEATH

If only for this life we have hope in Christ, we are to be pitied more than all men. But Christ has indeed been raised from the dead, the first-fruits of those who have fallen asleep. For since death came through a man, the resurrection of the dead comes also through a man. For as in Adam all die, so in Christ all will be made alive.

1 Corinthians 15:19–22

And I heard a loud voice from the throne saying, "Now the dwelling of God is with men, and he will live with them. They will be his people, and God himself will be with them and be their God. He will wipe every tear from their eyes. There will be no more death or mourning or crying or pain, for the old order of things has passed away."

Revelation 21:3–4

God's Words of Life on

GRIEF AND DEATH

Even though I walk
    through the valley of the shadow
      of death,
I will fear no evil,
    for you are with me, Lord;
your rod and your staff,
    they comfort me.

Psalm 23:4

If any of you lacks wisdom, he
should ask God, who gives generously to all without finding fault,
and it will be given to him.

James 1:5

"I will instruct you and teach you
in the way you should go;
I will counsel you and watch
over you," says the LORD.

Psalm 32:8

God's Words of Life on
GUIDANCE

Your word, O LORD, is a lamp
to my feet
and a light for my path.

Psalm 119:105

The Lord guides me in paths
of righteousness
for his name's sake.

Psalm 23:3

Dear friends, build yourselves up
in your most holy faith and pray in
the Holy Spirit. Keep yourselves
in God's love as you wait for the
mercy of our Lord Jesus Christ to
bring you to eternal life.

Jude 1:20–21

God's Words of Life on
HOLINESS

Therefore, I urge you . . . in view of God's mercy, to offer your bodies as living sacrifices, holy and pleasing to God—this is your spiritual act of worship. Do not conform any longer to the pattern of this world, but be transformed by the renewing of your mind. Then you will be able to test and approve what God's will is—his good, pleasing and perfect will.

Romans 12:1–2

An honest answer
is like a kiss on the lips.
Proverbs 24:26

A truthful witness saves lives.
Proverbs 14:25

Kings take pleasure in honest lips;
they value a man who speaks
the truth.
Proverbs 16:13

Truthful lips
endure forever.
Proverbs 12:19

Hope deferred makes the heart sick,
but a longing fulfilled is a tree
of life.

Proverbs 13:12

Know also that wisdom is sweet to
your soul;
if you find it, there is a future
hope for you,
and your hope will not be cut off.

Proverbs 24:14

And hope does not
disappoint us, because
God has poured out
his love into our hearts
by the Holy Spirit,
whom he has given us.

Romans 5:5

God's Words of Life on

HOSPITALITY

Share with God's people who are
in need. Practice hospitality.

Romans 12:13

When an alien lives with you in
your land, do not mistreat him.
The alien living with you must be
treated as one of your native-born.
Love him as yourself.

Leviticus 19:33–34

God's Words of Life on
HOSPITALITY

Share your food with the hungry
and . . . provide the poor
wanderer with shelter—
when you see the naked,
clothe him,
and [do not] turn away from
your own flesh and blood.
Then your light will break forth
like the dawn,

and your healing will quickly
appear;
then your righteousness will go
before you,
and the glory of the LORD will be
your rear guard.

Isaiah 58:7–8

God's Words of Life on
JOY

God will yet fill your mouth
    with laughter
    and your lips with shouts of joy.
Job 8:21

Light is shed upon the righteous
    and joy on the upright in heart.
Psalm 97: 11

You have made known
to me the path of life,
O Lord;
you will fill me with joy
in your presence,
with eternal pleasures
at your right hand.

Psalm 16:11

God's Words of Life on
JOY

Those who sow in tears
    will reap with songs of joy.
He who goes out weeping,
    carrying seed to sow,
will return with songs of joy,
    carrying sheaves with him.

Psalm 126:5–6

Good will come to him who is
generous and lends freely.

Psalm 112:5

Blessed is he who is kind to
the needy.

Proverbs 14:2 1

A generous man
will prosper;
he who refreshes
others will himself
be refreshed.

Proverbs 11:25

God is love.

1 John 4:8

God's Words of Life on
LOVE

Above all, love each other deeply, because love covers over a multitude of sins.

1 Peter 4:8

No one has ever seen God; but if we love one another, God lives in us and his love is made complete in us.

1 John 4:12

Jesus said, "Love each other as I
have loved you. Greater love has no
one than this, that he lay down his
life for his friends."

John 15:12–13

Be devoted to one another in
brotherly love. Honor one another
above yourselves.

Romans 12:10

God's Words of Life on
LOVE

Love is patient, love is kind. It does not envy, it does not boast, it is not proud. It is not rude, it is not self-seeking, it is not easily angered, it keeps no record of wrongs. Love does not delight in evil but rejoices with the truth.

1 Corinthians 13:4–6

Because of his great love for us,
God, who is rich in mercy, made us
alive with Christ even when we
were dead in transgressions—it is by
grace you have been saved.

Ephesians 2:4–5

Blessed are the merciful,
for they will be
shown mercy.

Matthew 5:7

Here is a trustworthy saying that deserves full acceptance: Christ Jesus came into the world to save sinners. . . . I was shown mercy so that in me, the worst of sinners, Christ Jesus might display his unlimited patience as an example for those who would believe on him and receive eternal life.

1 Timothy 1:15–16

God's Words of Life on
PEACE

Jesus said, "Peace I leave with you;
my peace I give you. I do not give
to you as the world gives. Do not
let your hearts be troubled and do
not be afraid."

John 14:27

I will lie down and sleep in peace,
for you alone, O LORD,
make me dwell in safety.

Psalm 4:8

May the Lord of peace himself
give you peace at all times and in
every way.

2 Thessalonians 3:16

The fruit of righteousness will
        be peace;
    the effect of righteousness will be
        quietness and confidence forever.

Isaiah 32:17

Your attitude should be the same as
that of Christ Jesus:
Who, being in very nature God, did
not consider equality with God
something to be grasped, but made
himself nothing, taking the very
nature of a servant, being made in
human likeness.

And being found in appearance as a
man, he humbled himself and
became obedient to death— even
death on a cross!
Therefore God exalted him to the
highest place and gave him the
name that is above every name.

Philippians 2:5–9

PERSPECTIVE

I will remember the deeds
  of the LORD;
    yes, I will remember your
      miracles of long ago. . . .
Your path led through the sea,
  your way through the
    mighty waters,
      though your footprints
        were not seen.

Psalm 77: 11, 19

When you pray, go into your room, close the door and pray to your Father, who is unseen. Then your Father, who sees what is done in secret, will reward you.

Matthew 6:6

"Call to me and I will answer you and tell you great and unsearchable things you do not know," says the Lord.

Jeremiah 33:3

God's Words of Life on
PRAYER

Jesus said, "Ask and it will be given to you; seek and you will find; knock and the door will be opened to you. For everyone who asks receives; he who seeks finds; and to him who knocks, the door will be opened."

Matthew 7:7–8

PRAYER

Let us . . . approach the throne of
grace with confidence, so that we
may receive mercy and find grace
to help us in our time of need.

Hebrews 4:16

God's Words of Life on
HIS PRESENCE

God has said,
"Never will I leave you;
never will I forsake you."
Hebrews 13:5

Jesus said, "Surely I am with you
always, to the very end of the age."
Matthew 28:20

God's Words of Life on
HIS PRESENCE

"So do not fear, for I am with you;
  do not be dismayed, for I am
    your God.
I will strengthen you and help you;
  I will uphold you with my right-
    eous right hand," says the Lord.

Isaiah 41:10

"Be still, and know that I am God."

Psalm 46:10

God's Words of Life on
RELATIONSHIPS

Be completely humble and gentle;
be patient, bearing with one another in love. Make every effort to
keep the unity of the Spirit through
the bond of peace.

Ephesians 4:2–3

RELATIONSHIPS

Bear with each other and forgive whatever grievances you may have against one another. Forgive as the Lord forgave you.

Colossians 3:13

Two are better than one,
    because they have a good return
      for their work:
If one falls down,
    his friend can help him up.
But pity the man who falls
    and has no one to help him up! . . .
Though one may be overpowered,
    two can defend themselves.
A cord of three strands is not
    quickly broken.

Ecclesiastes 4:9–10, 12

God's Words of Life on
REST

Jesus said, "Come to me, all you who are weary and burdened, and I will give you rest. Take my yoke upon you and learn from me, for I am gentle and humble in heart, and you will find rest for your souls. For my yoke is easy and my burden is light."

Matthew 11:28–30

God's Words of Life on
REST

Let the beloved of the LORD rest
secure in him,
for he shields him all day long,
and the one the LORD loves rests
between his shoulders.

Deuteronomy 33:12

SELF-WORTH

Do you not know that your body is a temple of the Holy Spirit, who is in you, whom you have received from God? You are not your own; you were bought at a price. Therefore honor God with your body.

1 Corinthians 6:19–20

God's Words of Life on
SELF-WORTH

For you created my inmost being,
   Lord;
   you knit me together in my
   mother's womb.
I praise you because I am fearfully
   and wonderfully made;
   your works are wonderful,
   I know that full well.

Psalm 139:13–14

Are not two sparrows sold for a penny? Yet not one of them will fall to the ground apart from the will of your Father. And even the very hairs of your head are all numbered. So don't be afraid; you are worth more than many sparrows.

Matthew 10:29–31

God's Words of Life on
SPEECH

Do not let any unwholesome talk
come out of your mouths, but only
what is helpful for building others
up according to their needs, that it
may benefit those who listen.

Ephesians 4:29

The lips of the righteous
nourish many.

Proverbs 10:21

Let your conversation be always
full of grace, seasoned with salt,
so that you may know how to
answer everyone.

Colossians 4:6

God's Words of Life on
TALENTS & ABILITIES

There are different kinds of gifts, but the same Spirit. There are different kinds of service, but the same Lord. There are different kinds of working, but the same God works all of them in all men. Now to each one the manifestation of the Spirit is given for the common good. To one there is given through the Spirit the message of wisdom, to another the message of knowledge by means of the same

TALENTS & ABILITIES

Spirit, to another faith by the same
Spirit, to another gifts of healing by
that one Spirit, to another miraculous
powers, to another prophecy, to
another distinguishing between spir-
its, to another speaking in different
kinds of tongues, and to still another
the interpretation of tongues. All
these are the work of one and the
same Spirit, and he gives them to
each one, just as he determines.

1 Corinthians 12:4–11

God's Words of Life on
THANKFULNESS

Therefore since we are receiving
a kingdom that cannot be shaken,
let us be thankful.

Hebrews 12:28

Praise the LORD.
Give thanks to the LORD,
    for he is good;
    his love endures forever.

Psalm 106:1

God's Words of Life on

THANKFULNESS

The LORD is my strength
  and my shield;
  my heart trusts in him,
  and I am helped.
My heart leaps for joy
  and I will give thanks
  to him in song.

Psalm 28:7

God's Words of Life on
TRUST

You will keep in perfect peace
  him whose mind is steadfast,
  because he trusts in you.
Trust in the LORD forever,
  for the LORD, the LORD,
  is the Rock eternal.

Isaiah 26:3–4

TRUST

Whoever gives heed to instruction
    prospers,
    and blessed is he who trusts
    in the LORD.

Proverbs 16:20

God's Words of Life on
TRUST

Trust in the LORD with all
       your heart
    and lean not on your own
       understanding;
in all your ways acknowledge him,
    and he will make your paths
       straight.

Proverbs 3:5–6

God's Words of Life on

VALUES

Who may ascend the hill
    of the LORD?
  Who may stand in his holy place?
He who has clean hands
    and a pure heart.

Psalm 24:3–4

The LORD rewards every man for
his righteousness and faithfulness.

1 Samuel 26:23

God's Words of Life on
VALUES

The LORD has rewarded me
    according to my righteousness,
according to the cleanness
    of my hands in his sight.

Psalm 18:24

Surely you desire truth
in the inner parts, Lord;
you teach me wisdom
in the inmost place.

Psalm 51:6

God's Words of Life on

WISDOM

If you accept my words
and store up my commands
within you,
turning your ear to wisdom
and applying your heart
to understanding,
and if you call out for insight
and cry aloud for understanding,
and if you look for it as for silver

Jesus will say, "Well done, good
and faithful servant! You have
been faithful with a few things;
I will put you in charge of many
things. Come and share your
master's happiness!"

Matthew 25 : 21

This book has been bound using
handcraft methods and Smyth-sewn
to ensure durability.

The dust jacket and interior were
designed by Maria Taffera Lewis.

The text was edited by
Pamela Liflander.

The text was set in Goudy and
Goudy Italic.